Drunk Every Sunday

A Study For Lent.

Pat Daily

Boundary Layer Books
Houston, Texas

Boundary Layer, Inc.
12115 Arcadia Bend Ln.
Houston, TX, 77041
pat@boundarylayerinc.com

The publisher cannot verify the accuracy or functionality of website URLs used in this book beyond the date of publication.

Cover design and image:
Interior design:
Editing: New Leaf Editorial Services, Rebecca Jones

ISBN 979-8-9866930-7-1 (print)
ISBN 979-8-9866930-8-8 (ebook)
ISBN 979-8-9866930-9-5 (audiobook)

Dedication

This book is dedicated to my wife, Ardith, who helped save my life and soul.

Contents

Introduction

Why the title?

Several years ago, we discussed Lent and fasting in our small group. I had just learned that Sundays are not counted in Lent. What else did I not know? I had ritually given things up for Lent for years with middling success. I tried to fast on Ash Wednesday and Good Friday with more failures than successes because I never spent the time to understand *why* we fast.

Some people give things up during Lent; some take on a discipline. One of the women in our class mentioned that her father would give up drinking. As a routine drinker, he had built up a tolerance for his alcohol consumption. Then, after the first week of Lent, he would drink again on Sunday. The problem was that in the preceding six days, his alcohol tolerance had significantly decreased. When he drank on Sundays in Lent, he drank the same amount as he would outside of Lent. He got *drunk every Sunday.* That story has stayed with me since.

This book is designed to begin on the Sunday before Ash Wednesday and conclude on the Sunday before Easter. It serves as a guide for individuals and small groups who wish to learn about and benefit from the season of Lent.

Along the way, I'll also point out where some Lenten practices, including mine, have gone astray.

Here's a quick joke as an example:

A man walks into a bar alone and orders three beers. The bartender finds this odd but complies with the request.

The man pays, takes the beers to a table, and drinks them one at a time, then leaves.

The following week, he returns to the bar and does the same. Three beers, drinks them alone, and leaves.

After three weeks, the bartender can no longer restrain his curiosity.

"Wouldn't it make more sense to order the beers one at a time? Then the second and third beers would be colder and fresher?"

"Certainly," the man agrees. "But for years, once a week, I would join my two brothers for a beer. Now they've moved away, but I do this in their memory."

"Ah," the bartender says. "Now I understand."

Several months later, the man orders only two beers. The bartender is curious, but doesn't question the man. However, when the man only orders two beers again the next week, the bartender has to ask.

"Since I first met you, you've always ordered three beers, yet these last two weeks, you've only ordered two. Why is that?"

"Well," the man replies, "I've given up drinking for Lent."

A History of Lent

Lent is a creation of people. It is not mentioned in the Bible and has been criticized by many since the Protestant Reformation. John Calvin wrote in 1536 that

> John Calvin is most remembered for his belief in predestination and that works alone were not sufficient for salvation.

Lenten practices were not an accurate imitation of Christ.[1] Some Protestant denominations practice it, and others do not. Over the years, there's been some heated rhetoric regarding Lent and how it is observed. Is there anything about Lent that can help us in our quest to draw closer to God and strengthen our faith?

Yes. But when, where, and how did Lent begin?

In 310 AD, the Roman Empire was in a state of chaos. Constantine, Maxentius, and Licinius all had claims to the empire, and civil wars raged. Christians were

---

[1] John Calvin, *Institutes of the Christian Religion* 4.12.20, accessed April 20, 2025, https://www.biblestudytools.com/history/calvin-institutes-christianity/book4/chapter-12.html.

persecuted in some quarters of the empire but tolerated in others.

The early Christian church was in no better shape. A tradition had arisen that converts were only to be baptized on Easter. These converts were expected to fast (one meal per day) for the forty days prior. Unbaptized Christians were considered "under instruction" and referred to as *catechumen* (derived from the Greek word for "one being instructed"). Some odd practices and heresies were arising involving baptism, ordination of clergy, self-castration, and the divinity of Christ, among others.

In 312 AD, on the eve of the Battle of Milvian Bridge, Constantine reportedly had a vision of a Chi-Rho and the words "In this sign, conquer." He had his soldiers paint Chi-Rhos on their shields. They won the battle, and Constantine "converted" to

Figure 1. The Chi-Rho is still widely used in the Catholic and Orthodox traditions.

Christianity. In Greek, chi and rho are the first two letters of *Christos*. Around this time, Constantine's mother, Helena (later Saint Helena), converted to Christianity and had a profound influence on her son and the Church.

The following year, in 313 AD, Emperor Constantine issued the Edict of Milan, which legalized Christianity and ended religious persecution. All religions were now legal in Rome. The next decade saw more turmoil, and Arianism arose as a heresy within the Church.

Arius was a Cyrenaic presbyter. Cyrene was a northeastern coastal town in what is now Libya. *Presbyter* was an honorific title for an elder in the early Church. Arius somehow decided that Jesus was not coeternal with God but was created by God before time. This is quite a spiritual rabbit hole, and I have my thoughts.

Constantine I issued the Edict of Milan in 313 AD, legalizing Christianity for Roman citizens shortly after his conversion. He reportedly refused to be baptized until near his death, supposedly because he believed he would have less time to corrupt his soul.

If something happens "before time," what does that even mean? How do you measure eternity, or coeternity, without time? Still, the argument raged and won't be definitively settled this side of death.

Arius considered and preached that Jesus was divine but not fully divine. Arius was exiled, but Arianism[2] was taking a strong hold in Egypt, notably in Alexandria.

By 324 AD, Constantine had had enough of the confusion and mixed practices between Christian communities. He convened the Council of Nicaea[3] to sort things out, particularly Arianism. The Council met in 325 AD and squashed Arianism, although some of its tenets exist today in the Jehovah's Witness theology. This rebuke resulted in the first version of the Nicene Creed. The contemporary version contains these words to help standardize the foundations of belief:

We believe in one Lord, Jesus Christ,
the only Son of God,
eternally begotten of the Father,
God from God, Light from Light,
true God from true God,
begotten, not made,
of one Being with the Father.[4]

---

[2] "Arius and Nicea," Fuller Seminary, accessed May 17, 2025, https://www.fuller.edu/next-faithful-step/resources/arius-and-nicea/.

[3] Looking at the canons published by the Council, you can see how confused the Church was at the time. These canons included the prohibition of self-castration by clergy; bishops, presbyters, and deacons were not to wander into neighboring cities to officiate; usury was prohibited by the clergy; and kneeling was forbidden on Sundays and during Pentecost.

[4] *The Book of Common Prayer* (Oxford University Press, 1990), 358. The emphasis is mine.

The Council is also credited with taking the first steps toward regularizing the emerging practice of Lent.

What's in a name? Originally, Lent was called Quadragesima, a Latin term meaning "fortieth." That makes sense for forty days, but where did *Lent* come from? The word stems from Old English *lencten,* which meant "spring season," or the Germanic *langatinez* ("long days").

The term *Lent* to refer to the 40 days (excluding Sundays) prior to Easter became standardized following the Second Vatican Council (1962–1965), when the traditional Latin Mass was translated into local languages, including English.

"Catholic History & Heritage: Vatican II," Carroll College, accessed May 21, 2025, https://www.carroll.edu/about/history/.

Today, it's very close to the Dutch *lente* and German *lenz.*

The Roman Catholic church transitioned to calling this period Lent when the Latin Mass was translated into English in 1964. The Old English version (*lencten*— "spring season") feels pagan, particularly in conjunction with the Latin word *Februa*: the root of the ancient Roman *February.*

Februa means "purification rites" and was a month of cleansing and sacrifices devoted to Februus, the god of purification. Humorously, Old English used *Solmonath*[5] for February, meaning "mud month." Depending on where you live, that may hit home during those rainy, dreary days before the beginning of spring. Even today, not everyone refers to it as Lent. The Italians, French, and Spanish stick with words closely related to *forty*. Slavic languages, such as Czech, use words like *Pust*, which can be translated as "fasting."

Longer days, forty days, fasting—take your pick. The word's roots remain murky, but the practices have crystallized. For the remainder of this book, we'll call this period *Lent*.

---

[5] Howard Suer, "The History of February History," *The Box City Bulletin*, accessed May 17, 2025, https://howardsuer.wordpress.com/2013/01/01/the-hi-s-tory-of-february-history-solmonath/.

Following the Council of Nicaea, Lent was formalized as a forty-day period. In 321 AD, Constantine named Sunday a day of rest—the Christian Sabbath. Early on, Sundays were still counted as part of Lent. It wasn't until Pope Gregory (590–604 AD) that Lent was formalized as the

> We know Christ was crucified and resurrected after eating the Passover meal with His disciples (Matt. 26:17–29).
>
> The Hebrew calendar is based on lunar cycles. The 15th day of Nisan always falls on a full moon, and Passover lasts eight days. The calculation of the Easter date is confusing but makes sense with what we know from the Scriptures.

forty-six days before Easter, and Sundays were not to be considered part of Lent. I get some of the logic here—Sundays are "mini-Easters" where we celebrate the Resurrection. Does it make sense to fast during a celebration? That's what got us to Ash Wednesday as the starting date. But what about Easter? Why does it move around?

Now on the first day of the Feast of the Unleavened Bread the disciples came to Jesus, saying to Him, "Where do You want us to prepare for You to eat the Passover?" (Matt. 26:17).

This ties the Last Supper and Christ's crucifixion and resurrection to the Jewish Passover feast.

The Hebrew calendar determines Passover, specifically the 15th of Nisan, which is the first month of the Hebrew year based on the lunar calendar.

Easter is the first Sunday after the first full moon that occurs on or after the spring equinox. Since time zones are somewhat arbitrary and some locations don't observe daylight savings time, the actual date of the equinox—that instant when Earth's celestial equator intersects with the center of the sun—can vary between March 19th and the 21st. Now, factor in the length of a lunar month (27 days, 7 hours, and 43 minutes to complete one orbit around Earth). But it takes about 29.5 days to go from full moon to full moon.

Confused yet? Me too, but remember that there were no universally recognized calendars when all this was set in motion. No one had GPS, smartphones, or the Weather Channel app, but everyone who could see the sky could figure out when the equinox occurred and when the first full moon happened. Agrarian societies lived by the seasons, planted by the seasons, and celebrated the transition from long, muddy winters to spring flowers. I think that early church leaders understood this and picked a date that was calculable by the average farmer, shepherd, or fisherman. Spring is the perfect time to celebrate the Resurrection.

Back to Ash Wednesday. The forty days became problematic once Pope Gregory decided that Sundays should be days of feasting rather than fasting. After all, Sundays are celebrations of the Resurrection, so why would we fast during a celebration central to our faith? Taking out the Sundays and backdating, Gregory chose a Wednesday and went from there.

Interestingly, Ramadan is also tied to a lunar calendar, but it is based on the first sighting of the crescent moon, not the full moon. In any case, Easter and Passover happen around the same time. Ramadan moves around.

The Bible doesn't give us any hints about a specific day of the year when Christ was born, and there are no handy references to Passover or other historical dates for

> Easter and Passover are tied together. Ramadan is tied to a different lunar calendar and moves significantly from year to year.

us to cling to. Christmas was set to December 25th based on the calculations of Sextus Julius Africanus, a second-century Christian historian. He determined that Gabriel announced to Mary that she would conceive Jesus on March 25th. Add nine months to that, and you have December 25th for Christmas.

As Christians, we honor our Hebrew roots by anchoring Easter to Passover. It makes the celebration of His resurrection move around, but that's okay with me.

Depending on your church, the altar may look different during Lent. Purple cloth is draped on the cross, symbolizing both royalty and penance — the royalty of Christ as King of Kings and our

> The original purple dye (Tyrian purple) was made from the mucus of sea snails and very expensive. In early Roman times, the color was reserved for emperors and senators.

call to repentance. On Good Friday, the cloth may be changed to black and then replaced with white on Easter. Mark 15:17–20 tells us that following Pilate's delivery of Christ for crucifixion, the soldiers dressed Him in purple and mocked Him as King of the Jews.

Christ never claimed this title Himself. The magi used it first in the book of Matthew:

Now after Jesus was born in Bethlehem of Judea in the days of Herod the king, behold, wise men from the East came to Jerusalem, saying, "Where is He who has been born King of the Jews? For we have seen His star in the East and have come to worship Him" (Matt. 2:1–2).

The magi calling Christ the King of the Jews tied him to the messianic prophecies of the Old Testament (such as Daniel 7:13–14).

Pilate used the title and had it inscribed above Christ on His cross (John 19:19).

One ritual whose origin is lost in time is the stripping of the altar after the Maundy Thursday (also called Holy Thursday in some traditions) services. Eamon Duffy's book, *The Stripping of the Altars*,[6] indicates that it was practiced as early as the 1400s. It involves removing everything except the cross and candle from altars without ceremony, usually performed by the clergy. Early versions also involved washing the altar and surrounding pavement. In the Vatican, the papal altar was washed with wine and water. Today, most churches simply strip the altar. Many Catholic, Lutheran, Methodist, and Anglican churches continue this tradition as a symbolic act representing the humiliation of Jesus and the abandonment of His disciples before His crucifixion.

Discussion

1. Are there Lenten traditions that confuse you? What are they?

2. Some Christians argue that Lent shouldn't be observed as it seems to set aside one block of time for repentance when we should continually repent for our sins. What do you think of this argument?

3. John Calvin disliked Lent because it wasn't an accurate "imitation of Christ." Should all aspects

---

[6] Duffy's book mentions the ritual almost in passing. Broadly, his book is more about Medieval Catholicism.

of Christianity be imitations of Christ? Why or why not?

Exercise

1. Try fasting. Ash Wednesday is a perfect day for it. Try to go without food from sundown on Tuesday until sundown on Ash Wednesday. Be sensible, and if you have a medical condition that precludes fasting from food, try a different kind of fast (TV, social media, etc.).

2. Spend some time in prayer contemplating how you observe Lent. Has it become just a ritual, or is it still rich in meaning to you?

SESSION 2

Ashes and Fasting

Ashes are mentioned frequently in the Bible and generally serve as a sign of humility before God and a symbol of repentance for sin. The first mention is in Genesis, when Abraham intercedes for Sodom. This section of the Bible always makes me smile when I think of Abraham arguing with God's plan. Abraham uses the term as a sign of his humility:

Then Abraham answered and said, "Indeed now, I who am but dust and ashes have taken it upon myself to speak to the Lord" (Gen. 18:27).

Isaiah 58:5–6 challenges us to think about what pleases God when we fast.

Are we showing off, or are we helping others?

The Ancient Near East—what most of us think of as the Middle East today—continues to have a tradition of visible displays of grief. Public wailing and tearing of clothes are not uncommon following the deaths of loved ones. Some scholars point to the linguistic roots of words we routinely translate as grief.

In Hebrew, grief has both emotional and behavioral aspects, and the word's roots are tied to outward behaviors as much as, if not more than, emotional states.[7] Grieving was expected to be visible to others. In the United States and much of Europe, mourners wear black to signify their emotional state.

Ashes also signify a lowly situation, as when Satan struck Job with boils (Job 2:7–8). Job then took a piece of broken pottery to scrape those boils as he sat in the ashes. Daniel hoped to turn God's wrath and prepared for this plea by fasting and wearing sackcloth and ashes:

Then I set my face toward the Lord God to make request by prayer and supplications, with fasting, sackcloth, and ashes. And I prayed to the Lord my God, and made confession, and said, "O Lord, great and awesome God, who keeps His covenant and mercy with those who love Him, and with those who keep His commandments, we have sinned and committed iniquity, we have done wickedly and rebelled, even by departing from Your precepts and Your judgments" (Dan. 9:3–6).

---

[7] David A. Bosworth, "Grief, Sadness, and Depression in the Hebrew Bible and Ancient Near East," *Oxford Research Encyclopedia of Religion* (May 22, 2024), accessed Feb. 26, 2025,
https://oxfordre.com/religion/view/10.1093/acrefore/978019934 0378.001.0001/acrefore-9780199340378-e-1190.
See also *The Semantic Dictionary of Biblical Hebrew* at: https://semanticdictionary.org.

Note how closely the prayer itself is reflected in variants of many denominations' prayer of confession, often recited before receiving Communion:

Merciful God, we confess that we have sinned against you in thought, word, and deed, by what we have done and what we have left undone. We have not loved You with our whole heart; we have not loved our neighbors as ourselves. We justly deserve Your judgment.

Jesus himself, when rebuking the impenitent cities in which He had done many mighty works, said:

"Woe to you, Chorazin! Woe to you, Bethsaida! For if the mighty works done in you had been done in Tyre and Sidon, they would have repented long ago in sackcloth and ashes" (Matt. 11:21 and Luke 10:13).

Why don't we wear sackcloth anymore?

Over time, sackcloth—like fasting—grew less prevalent. I'm not sure why, but I have some ideas.

Sackcloth was typically made of goat hair and is often thought of today as equivalent to burlap. Neither sound particularly comfortable and that was the point. People in mourning or wanting to prove their submission to God didn't want to be comfortable. The discomfort was an outward sign and an inward reminder of commitment.

These days, we love—and expect—comfort. I'm in my sixties and don't know anyone who has ever worn sackcloth. The closest thing I can recall is people wearing shirts made from flour sacks. They're not nearly as uncomfortable. Today, we wear black as a token of mourning. Does it now, or did it ever, matter to God?

God knows our hearts. I don't urinate or defecate outdoors. I wouldn't start now just because it was common in Christ's time. I'm also not going to start cooking my food over an open flame (except when camping and making s'mores). Maybe it's not just about discomfort and inconvenience. Could it also be an outward sign to others about where you are in life? An indication of your faith or loss invites communion and connection.

> Sackcloth is essentially the same thing as a "hair shirt."
> Today you can buy a burlap gown online for prices up to $1,000.

Still, ashes are a worthy way to begin our Lenten journey with humility and repentance. When they are imposed, the prayer reminds us to be humble by saying, "Remember that you are dust, and to dust you shall return," or "Repent and believe in the Gospel." The ashes remind us that we are sinners. The cross reminds us that we have a Savior.

Some critics consider the wearing of ashes hypocritical and contradictory to Matthew 6:16–18. This is a situation where intent matters. If you are repentant, humble,

> Jesus was welcomed into Jerusalem by a great multitude who took palm branches and went out to meet Him (John 12:12–13).
>
> In Rome, palm branches were used to symbolize victory for gladiators and emperors.

and sincerely attempting to commit to change and become better, then wearing ashes on one day out of the year is fine. It's when you want to use them to symbolize your piety and hope people will notice that you grow hypocritical.

One of the wonderful aspects of Lent is the continual connection to Easter. Many churches use the previous year's palm fronds to make the ashes imposed on Ash Wednesday. As you go through Lent—even when wearing ashes or fasting—remember that it's all about Easter and the Lord's resurrection.

Fasting

Christ expects us to fast. Matthew 6:16 begins with Christ saying, "Moreover, when you fast . . ." He didn't say *if* you fast. He said *when*. That's an important distinction.

One of the things I'm guilty of is giving up fasting too quickly. "I forgot that I was supposed to be fasting and had breakfast, so I just gave up."

If my children said something like that, I'd encourage them to try again and remind them that progress comes in small steps and that the most worthwhile endeavors are often the hardest. It always amazes me how easy I am on myself while being hard on others. I know fasting is good for me, both spiritually and physically.

Early fasts were strict: one meal per day after 3 p.m. and no meat, fish, or dairy for forty days in honor of Jesus's forty-day and forty-night fast in the desert.

Unlike Lent, fasting is biblical and mentioned in the Bible over seventy times. Why "over seventy" and not a precise number? Well, translations and versions vary, as do the books that some Christians consider biblical. The concept of fasting for forty days significantly predates Jesus's ministry. The first we hear of it is from Moses when he was called up the mountain:

So Moses went into the midst of the cloud and went up into the mountain. And Moses was on the mountain forty days and forty nights (Exod. 24:18).

And when he reminded Israel of their rebellions:

"When I went up into the mountain to receive the tablets of stone, the tablets of the covenant which the Lord made with you, then I stayed on the mountain forty days and

forty nights. I neither ate bread nor drank water" (Deut. 9:9).

Then Moses turned around and did it again. Twice.

"Then I took the two tablets and threw them out of my two hands and broke them before your eyes. And I fell down before the Lord, as at the first, forty days and forty nights; I neither ate bread nor drank water, because of all your sin which you committed in doing wickedly in the sight of the Lord, to provoke Him to anger" (Deut. 9:17–18. See also Deut. 9:22–25 and Exod. 34:1–2, 28).

Another major prophet, Elijah, fasted forty days and nights after fleeing from Jezebel, following God's impressive rebuke of Baal (1 Kings 19:5–8).

> The Bible only mentions Christ fasting once. As an observant Jew, He would also have fasted two days per week, as He mentions in the Parable of the Pharisee and the Tax Collector in Luke 18:12.

When Jesus was led by the Spirit into the wilderness to be tempted, He started with a fast of forty days and nights. The Bible says that, following this fast, He was hungry (Matt. 4:1–11). I become hungry and unpleasant to be around when I miss breakfast. Imagine surviving forty days and nights with nothing. A quick internet search led me to conclude that most people would die after three days without water and three weeks without food. God sustained Moses, Elijah, and Jesus as they prepared for their ministries. I could survive Pope Gregory's forty-day fast (one meal per day after 3 p.m.), but even that would be trying.

Although not driven by Lent, other religions also observe fasting. Muslims fast from sunrise to sunset for the twenty-nine to thirty days of Ramadan. Jews observe two major, twenty-five-hour fasts and other minor sunrise-to-sunset fasts throughout the year. Buddhists, Hindus, and Baha'is also fast.

In time, Lent went from being a time of just fasting to something much more. For early Christians, Easter was the day when new converts were baptized, and it was they who observed fasting. Gradually, the fasting practice went from converts to all Christians. If you choose to fast, start with a simple approach: one meal per day, preferably in the afternoon or evening. Drink plenty of water, and follow the guidance found in Matthew 6:16–18:

Moreover, when you fast, do not be like the hypocrites, with a sad countenance. For they disfigure their faces that they may appear

> Fast with intention. Know why you are doing it. It shouldn't be simply for tradition or to show off your piety.

to men to be fasting. Assuredly, I say to you, they have their reward. But you, when you fast, anoint your head and wash your face, so that you do not appear to men to be fasting, but to your Father who is in the secret place;

and your Father who sees in secret will reward you openly.

Physically, fasting has tremendous payoffs. Interestingly, the method that seems to benefit most is a slight variation of Pope Gregory's (one meal daily after 3 p.m.). We now refer to this as intermittent fasting—reducing the amount of time and food consumed per day. While fasting, you should still drink water. Here are several examples of intermittent fasting:

- 16/8 method: Fast for sixteen hours each day and restrict your eating to a single eight-hour window. Please note that consuming 8,000 calories between 8 a.m. and 4 p.m. probably won't benefit you.

- 20/4 method: Same as above, but you limit your daily food intake to a four-hour window.

- One meal a day is consumed within one hour in the evening.

- 5:2 method: Eat normally for five days each week, but set aside two days to eat only one meal of about 600 calories.

Johns Hopkins Medicine[8] says that the benefits of this type of fasting may include:

- Improved memory and cognitive ability
- Heart health—improved blood pressure and resting heart rate
- Physical performance—fat loss while maintaining muscle mass
- Weight loss, reduced fasting glucose, and fasting insulin levels

If you have medical issues, fasting might not be your best choice. Talk to your doctor.

What about the spiritual benefits of fasting? I'm confident that God wants us to be healthy (3 John 1:2), but is that why fasting is mentioned so often in the Bible, just to keep us healthy? No. There are more important benefits when you fast with spiritual intent:

- Your focus moves from "What's for lunch?" to praying and listening for God's voice.
- Resisting food for a short period improves self-control and strengthens resistance to other types

---

[8] "Intermittent Fasting: What is it, and how does it work?" Johns Hopkins Medicine, accessed February 19, 2025, https://www.hopkinsmedicine.org/health/.

of temptation. "If I can do without breakfast and lunch, I can do without scrolling social media."

- Moves you from food reliance to Spirit reliance.

- Builds compassion and empathy for others. Some people fast because food is limited or not available—a difficult concept to understand when you live in a land of plenty. The United Nations[9] estimates that one out of every eleven people worldwide experience true hunger, not the slightly peckish feeling you get when you eat lunch an hour later than normal. Feeling a little hungry may move us to help others who routinely feel the pangs of insufficient food.

- Increases gratitude for what you have.

- Connects you to religious traditions and Christ's expectations.

John Wesley strongly advocated fasting as a regular spiritual discipline. Initially, he advocated two weekly fasts (Wednesday and Friday) following the one-meal-a-day model. Later, he advocated Friday fasting for Methodists, similar to the Anglican rule. In his Sermon 27, he addressed the natural basis of fasting: when people are so overwhelmed by events or emotions that they forget to eat.

---

[9]"Global Issues: Food," United Nations, accessed February 19, 2025, https://www.un.org/en/global-issues/food.

One who is under deep affliction, overwhelmed with sorrow for sin, and a strong apprehension of the wrath of God, would, without any rule, without knowing or considering whether it were a command of God or not, "forget to eat his bread," abstain not only from pleasant but even from needful food.

Modern Christians fast far less often than Christians did years ago.
What has driven that change?
Is the change beneficial?

Consider Paul's (then Saul) conversion on the road to Damascus (Acts 9:1–9) when Jesus spoke to him and asked Saul why he was persecuting Him. The scripture tells us that after his conversation with Jesus, Saul "was three days without sight, and neither ate nor drank" (Acts 9:9). Imagine how you might react after a close encounter with an unhappy Jesus. I would likely be off my feed for quite a while.

More recently, we have begun using the term *fasting* to refer to many types of abstinence. The concept, though, is well established. In a 1622 sermon, Saint Francis de Sales advocated keeping your eyes downcast when fasting so as not to look "upon frivolous and unlawful objects." He also recommended keeping the ears from hearing "vain talk, which serves only to fill the mind with worldly images." His parishioners were also advised to keep their tongues from speaking idle words.

Social media, anyone?

You may want to add other types of fasting to your spiritual discipline. Here are a few:

- Social media
- Unhealthy food
- Alcohol
- Television

Fasting is not easy. It's not supposed to be. While we shouldn't make a spectacle of our fasting, it may help you to have a fasting partner

> Fasting is about more than just giving up a few meals.

who can support you and empathize with your feelings. Don't take it out on others if you get cranky or "hangry" when you fast. Use that emotion as a reminder of what you're doing and why.

One last thought on fasting comes from Isaiah 58:6–7:

The kind of fasting I want is this: remove the chains of oppression and the yoke of injustice, and let the oppressed go free. ²Share your food with the hungry and open your homes to the homeless poor. Give clothes to those who have nothing to wear, and do not refuse to help your own relatives.[10] *(GNT)*

Discussion

1. If you've attempted a fast before and "failed," what caused the failure?

2. Consider those chained by oppression (see Isaiah above); how would you characterize their oppression? What can you do as a group (or class) or an individual to help remove their chains?

Exercise

If you're fasting, give away your breakfast and lunch. Make a bag with food and water to give to someone in need in your community.

---

[10] The Good News Translation is used here. It reads more powerfully than the NKJ version I usually use.

SESSION 3

Forty Days

The number 40 shows up in the Bible over 120 times. "Forty days and forty nights" shows up twenty-four times. Why is 40 so important to God? There's no clear answer in the Bible. Even the book of Numbers doesn't have a verse to explain it.[11] Some instances may be allegorical or metaphorical, while others are specific, exact measures of time. For whatever reason, forty days symbolize several things in the Bible: testing, trial, or completion.

> What's so special about the number 40?

When researching Lent, many books say it mimics Christ's days of temptation in the desert.[12] Remember, though, He didn't take Sundays off. *Forty* is used elsewhere in the Bible for various reasons. The first time

---

[11] Sorry. I couldn't resist this. Numbers is called that because it opens with a detailed census of the tribes of Israel—not because it explains why the Bible is full of repeated numbers.

[12] One of the many things that strikes me about the fasts of Jesus, Moses, and Elijah is that they didn't get Sundays off. There were no "cheat days" in their fasts. During Lent, Sundays take on a much greater significance for me than they do the rest of the year.

we see it is in Genesis 7:4, when God directed Noah's preparations for the flood.

"For after seven more days I will cause it to rain on the earth forty days and forty nights, and I will destroy from the face of the earth all living things that I have made."

Moses spent 40 days and 40 nights receiving the Ten Commandments on Mt. Sinai. The Israelites wandered in the desert for 40 years. Christ spent 40 days and nights fasting in the wilderness, and "afterward He was hungry" (Matt. 4:2).

What's most interesting to me is that Satan appeared to tempt Jesus *after* he'd fasted. That's precisely when you would expect someone's resistance to be at its lowest.

Why did Christ fast? John had just baptized Him. Even the Holy Spirit showed up, and God Himself spoke. That would seem to be the perfect time to start His ministry. Yet the Spirit led Him into the wilderness "to be tempted by the devil" (Matt. 4:1). I think God was demonstrating to us that His Son was fully human. God, in His perfection, cannot be tempted, yet our Savior could while He was on Earth. That proves that humans can resist temptation, and Matthew 4:4 reminds us that "Man shall not live by bread alone, but by every word that proceeds from the mouth of God."

Throughout the Bible, the number 40 symbolizes a testing, trial, or probation period and represents a transformation or a new beginning. As mentioned, early Christian converts were expected to fast for the 40 days before Easter, when they would be baptized into the Church. Lent represents an opportunity to use those 40 days for self-examination.

Self-examination

In his second letter to the Corinthians, Paul said:

Examine yourselves as to whether you are in the faith. Test yourselves. Do you not know yourselves, that Jesus Christ is in you?—unless indeed you are disqualified. But I trust that you will know that we are not disqualified (2 Cor. 13:5–6).

In his first letter to the same church, he advised self-examination in preparation for the Lord's Supper (1 Cor. 11:28–32).

Exercise: Read Psalms 139 and 1 Peter 3:10–11 and consider how they apply to you.

What does it mean to examine yourself, and how should we, as Christians trying to be better, go about it? A good place to start might be with our confessional prayer. When we confess that "we have sinned against you in thought, word, and deed, by what we have done and what we have left undone," what exactly are we confessing to? Let's start with the sins of thought.

How can a thought be a sin?

Read Proverbs 24:9. Depending on your Bible, the translation

Can a thought be a sin?

may be *The devising of foolishness is sin, and the scoffer is an abomination to men* (NKJV), or *The schemes of folly are sin, and people detest a mocker* (NIV).

Jesus Christ, in the Sermon on the Mount, said, *"But I say to you that whoever looks at a woman to lust for her has already committed adultery with her in his heart"* (Matt. 5:28).

President Jimmy Carter admitted to this in a 1976 interview with Playboy magazine during his campaign. He was roundly mocked for it and later said it almost cost him the election. The man admitted to a sin identified explicitly by Christ and became the target of nearly endless jokes.

I'll admit I'm as guilty of this sin as Carter was.

So, is any thought contrary to God's vision for us a sin? Maybe, but maybe not. Like fasting hypocritically, I think the intent has much to do with it. Everyone sins, and everyone has sinful thoughts—not just sexually oriented thoughts, but also thoughts of malice toward others, excessive pride, greed or covetous thoughts, and wrathful thoughts. I don't speak for any faith or congregation, but I believe that if a thought is fleeting, it might not rise to the level of a sin. When you spend time with it, watering the seed and tending its soil, it becomes a problem.

Sinning by word

"Sticks and stones may break my bones, but words shall never hurt me." Those are words we teach our children as a defense against name-calling and bullying. They're worth trying to employ ourselves. Still, can what you say be a sin? Certainly.

If you intend to harm someone or damage their reputation, incite others to violence, or curse the Lord, as Job's wife urged him to do, then those thoughts and words become a sin. After Satan had afflicted Job with boils, this exchange transpired between Job and his wife:

Then his wife said to him, "Do you still hold fast to your integrity? Curse God and die!"

But he said to her, "You speak as one of the foolish women speaks. Shall we indeed accept good from God, and shall we not accept adversity?" In all this Job did not sin with his lips (Job 2:9–10).

We wound people—other children of God—by the words we speak and write. Anyone with a social media account has seen some of the truly horrific things people say to others online. Drive in Houston during rush hour, and you can often see these sins. Even if you can't hear the words, you can read their lips and interpret their accompanying hand gestures. Sometimes, I think that I'm

> Are there unforgivable sins?

a better Christian toward strangers than I am toward my family. Over the years, I've said hurtful things to my wife and our children. I consider that a sin.

Here's a bigger one: blasphemy.[13] Christ said this in Matthew 12:31–32:

"Therefore I say to you, every sin and blasphemy will be forgiven men, but the blasphemy against the Spirit will not be forgiven men. Anyone who speaks a word against the Son of Man, it will be forgiven him; but whoever speaks against the Holy Spirit, it will not be forgiven him, either in this age or in the age to come."

Read that verse again. It's a wake-up call for anyone denying Christ. There are lots of resources available to help you understand what blasphemy against the Holy Spirit means, and I urge you to look for them and discuss this in class or church. My dictionary defines *blasphemy* as "the act or offense of speaking sacrilegiously about God or sacred things; profane talk."[14] Where this gets confusing to me is the concept that we can be forgiven for

---

[13] It may be a sin to commit blasphemy, but not a crime. There are countries where blasphemy is both and actually carries the death penalty: Mauritania, parts of Nigeria, Saudi Arabia, Yemen, Somalia, Iran, Afghanistan, Pakistan, and Qatar to name a few. "IRFBA Statement on Blasphemy and Related Offences," U.S. Department of State, accessed April 13, 2025, https://2021-2025.state.gov/irfba.

[14] *The Oxford American College Dictionary* (G. P. Putnam's Sons, 2002), under "blasphemy."

blaspheming Christ, but not the Holy Spirit. Aren't they all part of the Trinity? Father, Son, and Holy Spirit?

Yes. This was another thing that the Council of Nicaea formalized in 325 AD. It had long been a part of Christian tradition since Christ spoke the words reflected in Matthew 28:19–20:

"Go therefore and make disciples of all the nations, baptizing them in the name of the Father and of the Son and of the Holy Spirit, teaching them to observe all things that I have commanded you; and lo, I am with you always, even to the end of the age."

So, back to blasphemy of the Holy Spirit. The best explanation I found

> I am with you always, even to the end of the age.
> (Matt. 28:20)

comes from Focus on the Family, which states that it is essentially the sin of rejecting Christ.

"By continually rejecting God's free gift of salvation in Jesus, a sinner sears his conscience (ignores the voice of the Holy Spirit) and stiffens his neck. Eventually, he gets to the place where genuine repentance is no longer possible.

This stubborn and unrepentant attitude—persistent self-hardening—is the chief mark of true blasphemy against the Holy Spirit."[15]

If you're reading this, you're probably not guilty of this sin. I believe that even those who intentionally turn their backs on God can be forgiven this sin if they repent and accept the salvation offered by Christ.

Thoughts beget words, and words beget deeds.

You probably don't need a list of sinful actions, so let's consider the sins of "things left undone."

Most days, I feel I'm doing well since I haven't harmed anyone. That's comforting, but it's also incomplete.

Christ gave us guidance to love and help others:

". . . for I was hungry and you gave Me food; I was thirsty and you gave Me drink; I was a stranger and you took Me in; I was naked and you clothed Me; I was sick and you visited Me; I was in prison and you came to Me"* (Matt. 25:35–36).

When the righteous claimed they never saw the Lord in any of these circumstances, Jesus answered,

---

[15] "Blasphemy of the Holy Spirit and the Unforgivable Sin," Focus on the Family, accessed January 19, 2025, https://www.focusonthefamily.com/family.

"Assuredly, I say to you, inasmuch as you did it to one of the least of these My brethren, you did it to Me" (Matt. 25:40).

Ouch. What keeps us from helping others? Laziness? Lack of resources? Giving elsewhere? I've scoured

> What stops us from helping others?

my Bible for a verse that says, "It's okay to walk past someone in need as long as you're tithing to the church." It's not there. What is in the Bible is simple and nicely summed up in John 13:34–35 when Christ said:

"A new commandment I give to you, that you love one another; as I have loved you, that you also love one another. By this all will know that you are My disciples, if you have love for one another."

I think there's another thing that stops us from helping: *fear.* In the Parable of the Good Samaritan (Luke 10:25–37), the priest and the Levite passed by the battered, "half-dead" man. Why? They were afraid. Afraid of becoming ritually unclean. Perhaps even fearful of becoming personally entangled with the man.

A while ago, I was driving down a major road in Houston. Traffic began moving toward the shoulder, and I saw a man standing in the road. He was screaming at traffic and making rude gestures with both hands. At his feet, his bicycle blocked one lane of traffic.

He seemed uninjured but undoubtedly distressed. I pulled into a parking lot and called the police. The man got back on his bicycle and rode against traffic until he arrived at a restaurant. His behavior continued to be erratic, and I prayed that the police would come and help him. It took me thirty minutes to overcome my fear and help the man myself. Why? I was afraid—afraid that he might be violent, and I was alone.

My fear was unfounded. The man was polite and happy to accept help.

I'm not advocating that we should all run into potential danger. Do what you can, when and where you can. It helps to have a friend with you. Ecclesiastes 4:9–10 makes the point that two are better than one. It's even better to trust the Lord and remember that God is with us.

"Peace I leave with you, My peace I give to you; not as the world gives do I give to you. Let not your heart be troubled, neither let it be afraid" (John 14:27).

Discussion

1. When have you passed by someone who needed help? Why didn't you help? What could you have done differently?

2. In the Sermon on the Mount (Matt. 5:33–37), Jesus forbids oaths, saying that we should let our "Yes" be "Yes" and our "No" be "No." What does that mean, and how can we live by it?

Exercise

1. Create manna bags to keep in your car and give to those in need. Get a list of helping ministries from your church so that, if nothing else, you can point a needy soul in the right direction. If manna bags are new to you, here's a suggestion for how to build them: Start with a plastic bag. Throw in some bottled water, packaged nuts, dried fruit, meat sticks, and a protein or meal bar, and you're good to go. Feel free to adapt to your local needs and conditions.

2. Find some private time and consider your sins. Write them down. Make sure you have extra paper (I needed several sheets). Repent and resolve to be better. Pray for forgiveness and burn the paper. You've handed those sins over to Christ. Move on.

SESSION 4

Prayer

Prayer is mentioned over 650 times in the Bible. If you're looking for an indication that something is essential to your relationship with God, there it is. Lent is the perfect opportunity to start or reinvigorate your prayer life.

> Your prayers don't need to be lengthy, but they should be thoughtful. There are appropriate times for memorized prayer. There are also times for heartfelt pleas to the Lord.

We first see prayer mentioned in Genesis following the birth of Enosh (son of Seth):

Then men began to call on the name of the lord (Gen. 4:26).

The last prayer is nearly the last line in my Bible and comes from Revelation 22:20:

Even so, come, Lord Jesus!

I'm a father, and one of the greatest joys in my life is when my daughters call. My kids lead busy lives, so I worry that calling them will be inconvenient. If I called them every time I thought of them, they'd spend all their time on the phone with me. I believe God feels a Father's joy when we call Him in prayer.

When should we pray?

Anytime. The line is always open. Paul said:

Rejoice always, pray without ceasing, in everything give thanks; for this is the will of God in Christ Jesus for you (1 Thess. 5:16–18).

Jesus prayed:

- Before eating (Matthew 26:26 and Luke 24:30–31 are a couple of many examples.)
- Before making important decisions (Luke 6:12–13)
- Before healing (Mark 7:34–35)
- After healing (Luke 5:16)

Many people only pray when they're in distress. I'm sure God hears those prayers as clearly as others, but I think He'd like to hear from us even when things are going well.

How should we pray?

As a child, I knelt by my bed to say my prayers. In the church we attended, we knelt to pray. In 1 Kings 8:54, Solomon rises from kneeling before the altar while he prayed. Psalms 95:6 says:

Oh come, let us worship and bow down; Let us kneel before the lord our Maker.

What did Jesus do?

In Luke 22:41, Jesus knelt to pray in the garden of Gethsemane:

And He was withdrawn from them about a stone's throw, and He knelt down and prayed . . .

Christ also prayed while standing before the tomb of Lazarus (John 11:38–44) and looking up to Heaven in Mark 6:41 and Mark 7:34.

> When was the last time you knelt to pray?

Kneeling is a position of submission and surrender. When Christ knelt and prayed in the garden, He asked to be spared the cross but subjected Himself entirely to God's will.

The Council of Nicaea had some thoughts on prayer. They forbade kneeling to pray on Sundays and during Pentecost. Those were times of celebration.

Why do we clasp our hands together when we pray? Some suggest it's a position of pleading and submission. That makes sense. Some people pray with their hands out and palms up, forming the shape of the letter *Y*. This position is called the *orans* position, derived from the Latin word for "praying," and has roots in antiquity. It was the traditional posture of early Christian prayer when the entire church would stand in this position to pray. It may symbolize a beseeching and thankful orientation toward God. Psalms 63:4 says *I will lift up my hands in Your name.* And Psalms 143:6 states *I spread out my hands to You.* [16]

The Bible does not mandate a body position for prayer. As I've gotten older, I kneel less but pray more. I think what's most important is what is in your heart. If you must remind yourself to submit entirely to the Lord, kneeling may be appropriate. I like to remember C. S. Lewis's thoughts on prayer. He thought that both the body and soul should pray, and he did most of his praying on his knees. He also had this to say:

"Kneeling does matter, but other things matter even more. A concentrated

What does it really mean to "pray without ceasing" (1 Thess. 5:17)?

mind and a sitting body make for better prayer than a kneeling body and a mind half asleep."[17]

I smiled when I read that. For a while, I tried to pray after I got in bed and turned out the lights. Many of those

---

[16] My father was a lifelong Catholic. The first time my sister took him to an evangelical church, partway through the service he raised one hand in praise and waved it back and forth. Afterwards, my sister asked him about it. He said that he thought people in the choir were waving to him.

[17] C. S. Lewis, *Letters to Malcolm* (1964), 17.

nights the sum total of my prayer was "Heavenly Father... zzz." Lewis has a great point. A prayer said when alert is more likely to be complete and coherent.

Beyond your body's physical position, some other attributes lend themselves to effective prayer. By this, I don't mean that God grants your prayer, but that these characteristics help you open your heart to God and clarify your reason for a particular prayer. The Canaanite woman in Matthew 15:22–28 gives a nice example of praying with confidence, perseverance, and humility. She prays to Jesus for mercy because a demon was possessing her daughter. She was not a Jew, yet she already had enough faith in Christ to be confident that He could heal her daughter. When Christ initially ignores her, possibly to test her faith, she persists and comes to worship Him, saying, " 'Lord, help me!' " (Matt. 15:25).

Christ tests her again, seeming to say that what He has to offer is only for the Jews, and to give it to the Gentiles would be like taking food away from children to feed it to dogs (Matt. 15:26). That verse has always felt a bit harsh to me. Still, Christ is using this woman to make a point to both His disciples and the world. He was promised to the people of Israel and would be their salvation for those who accepted Him. The Canaanite woman perseveres again and humbles herself, saying that even dogs eat the crumbs that fall from their master's table (Matt. 15:27). Jesus makes His point by allowing the woman to argue. He heals the woman's daughter and calls her faith great (Matt. 15:28). He is here to save us all, Jews and Gentiles, and His grace will not be withheld.

There are a lot of prayer methods. I've followed the ACTS method on and off over the years and still like it, but it's just a prompt:

> Prayer methods such as ACTS or PRAY can help you organize your conversation with God.

A—Adoration. To me, this means reveling in the glory of God and His creation. Now and then, I try to make or repair something—raised flower beds, plumbing, storage bins, whatever. It's frustrating, and I appreciate tradespeople who do things right the first time. When I pray, I like to think about all the bits and pieces God had to put together to make the universe work and to make it all beautiful. The glory of a sunset is not an accident. That inspires my awe.

C—Contrition. I mess up a lot and have plenty to repent for. God already knows what we've done (or left undone). This part of prayer is about admitting our failures, putting them into words, and acknowledging them. Pro tip: This can be a short list if you pray often.

T—Thanksgiving. We've been given life. When I was younger, I never prayed about my health. (Mostly, it was good enough that I never really thought about it.) That's different now. I'm thankful for my health, the health of my family as well as people around the world, and even the health of my pets. There are beautiful trees, flowers, sunrises, and sunsets. There are warm days and cool ones to help us mark the passage of the seasons. The list here is almost endless.

S—Supplication. This is why most people pray; they want something from God. That's completely okay, but He probably enjoys hearing from you when things are going well, too. Ask away. Be confident. Persevere. Be humble. Always remember that while God answers all prayers, that answer is often "no." When Jesus prayed in the garden, He had a big ask of His Father:

. . . He knelt down and prayed, saying, "Father, if it is Your will, take this cup away from Me; nevertheless not My will, but Yours, be done" (Luke 22:41–42).

God must have wept to hear this from His Son. Then, in verses 43 and 44, we get a glimpse into how intensely Jesus prayed, to the point that His Father sent an angel to strengthen Him.

And being in agony, He prayed more earnestly. Then His sweat became like great drops of blood falling down to the ground (Luke 22:44).

This exemplifies the fully human aspect of Christ. He was afraid and knew that the next few days were going to be humiliating and brutally painful. He must have known that His own mother would be at the cross and would watch Him die. We only hear His words before the angel appeared. I think that with that additional strength, He moved on to the other things He knew would follow His death and resurrection—the brutal deaths of His disciples, the persecution of early Christians, and the stumbling of the church and Christians to this day.

Jesus was sent for our salvation, which couldn't happen without the cross, yet God's beloved Son asked if there was another way. The end of Christ's prayer is crucial: *"... not My will, but Yours, be done."* Even as He asked for a way to be spared His upcoming scourging and crucifixion, Jesus knew that He had to subject Himself to His Father's will. We must remember this when God seems silent in response to our prayers. Maybe there's a reason He won't get you out of that speeding ticket.

Another method is PRAY—Praise, Repent, Ask, Yield. It hits the points of the Lord's Prayer (Matt. 6:9–13).

> Praying can become a good habit. The more you do it, the easier and more natural it becomes.

These methods are great for adding a little structure if you tend to wander in your prayer, as I do. They help you get back on track. When you have time for longer prayers, they work great. The Bible doesn't give us a format for more extended prayer. And there are lots of other methods you can try. Sometimes, the prayer formulas hinder me, and I think, *I don't have time for all this right now.* It's as if I think the Lord needs a five-page essay prayer every time. Often, the short and sweet method is best. You lift your immediate thoughts to the Father:

"Lord, thank You for this beautiful sunrise."

"Heavenly Father, thank You for not letting Buster poop in the neighbor's yard again, and thank You for making sure I had a bag on hand."

"Please, Jesus, let the people in that car wreck be okay."

My impression of God—inspired by nothing more than my own life—is that He might prefer the bullet points spread out throughout the day, when they're on your heart, to a formulaic recitation that leaves out some important things.

The more often you open your heart to God, the easier it becomes.

Jesus taught us to pray by example. He even gave us an example in the Lord's Prayer (Matt. 6:9–13). He also prayed for Himself, His disciples, and us in John 17. What strikes me most about this is what He wanted for us. He didn't pray for us to be happy, healthy, or wealthy. He prayed for us to be with Him and the Father:

"I do not pray for these alone, but also for those who will believe in Me through their word; that they all may be one, as You, Father, are in Me, and I in You; that they also may be one in Us, that the world may believe that You sent Me"(John 17:20–21).

Please remember that prayer should not be one-sided, not just a laundry list of things you

> Make time in your prayer life to listen for God's answers.

want. You need to be quiet and listen for the "still, small voice" that spoke to Elijah. This is often the hardest thing for me to do; banishing the myriad aspects of daily life from your mind so that you can pay attention to the Lord requires time and discipline.

In Session 3, I told a story about being afraid to help a man on the street. I don't think I'm a typically anxious or fearful person. Even so, just as we were making a major change in our lives, my wonderful wife gave me a copy of this prayer by Saint Francis de Sales. I have reviewed it hundreds of times since then:

"Do not look forward in fear to the changes in life; rather, look to them with full hope as they arise. God, whose very own you are, will lead you safely through all things, and when you cannot stand it, God will carry you in His arms.

Do not fear what may happen tomorrow; the same understanding Father who cares for you today will take care of you then and every day.

He will either shield you from suffering or will give you unfailing strength to bear it. Be at peace and put aside all anxious thoughts and imaginations."

If you do only one thing this Lent, expand your prayer life and spend more quality time with the Savior.

Discussion

1. Read John 14:13–14. What does it mean to ask/pray for something in Jesus's name?

2. Read Exodus 2:23–25. The Israelites groaned in their slavery. God heard their groans. Does this make groaning about things a type of prayer?

3. Read Romans 8:26. Does that change your mind about the previous question?

Exercise

1. When someone cuts you off in traffic or is rude to you at Starbucks, try to pray for both of you. Open your heart to consider what trials they may be going through. Ask the Lord for help controlling your anger.

2. Make a special effort to add some quiet time at the end of your prayer to open your heart and mind to God.

The Two Great Commandments

Most Christians can easily recall Christ's answer when questioned by the scribe about what was the great commandment:

"'You shall love the lord your God with all your heart, with all your soul, and with all your mind.' This is the first and great commandment. And the second is like it: 'You shall love your neighbor as yourself.' On these two commandments hang all the Law and the Prophets" (Matt. 22:37–40).

The first verse about loving God is straightforward. I've never heard anyone try to parse

> Is everyone our neighbor? Even those we disagree with?

it too much—even if, as imperfect humans, we routinely fail to follow it (albeit unintentionally). It's the second commandment that gets our dander up—that bit about loving our neighbor as we do ourselves. Like the lawyer in Luke 10:29, we want some clarity.

Just who—exactly—is our neighbor?

The Parable of the Good Samaritan (Luke 10:30–37) tells of a man who is attacked on the road between Jerusalem and Jericho by thieves who strip him of his clothes and beat him nearly to death. Later, a priest sees the man, but instead of helping, he crosses to the other side of the road. Then, a Levite does the same thing. Finally, a Samaritan sees the man and helps him by taking him to an inn and treating his wounds. The Samaritan goes so far as to pay the innkeeper to care for the injured man and promises to pay more if necessary when he returns.

Christ puts the lawyer on the spot, asking:

"So which of these three do you think was neighbor to him who fell among the thieves?" (Luke 10:36).

The lawyer admits that it was the Samaritan.

Sometimes, we let the priest and the Levite off the hook by claiming they were worried about becoming ritually impure. That's true, but is it a sufficient justification to withhold aid?

The story is more profound because of the long-standing animosity between Jews and Samaritans. Before telling this tale, Jesus had been rejected by a Samaritan village. This angered John and James to the point that they wanted to rain fire down on the village (Luke 9:51–55). But in verse 56, Jesus reminds them:

"For the Son of Man did not come to destroy men's lives but to save them."

We need to remember that the next time we're full of righteous indignation. Christ's point is clear: Everyone

> Don't let judgment, prejudice, or bigotry get in the way of loving your neighbor.

is our neighbor, and everyone should be loved. Yes, I believe that God wants us to love every single human being regardless of . . . well, anything. That means people with different skin colors, different sexual preferences, different concepts of what *gender* means, different religious beliefs, different nationalities, and even those with —*gasp*— different political views. There is absolutely no biblical mandate to agree with everyone; quite the contrary, we are to love all.

Recently, I learned of a Bible study group in an uproar. A couple of highly opinionated members were condemning those outside their belief system. "All those _____ (fill in the blank with the group you hate most) are going straight to Hell." We are quicker to hate than to love, but love is the calling.

Last week, I made the mistake of scrolling through social media and stumbled across a full-blown firefight over who should be helped first when many are in need.

Some believe our love should be doled out like the ripples from a rock dropped in a pond: first and most to those nearest us, then what remains can spread to those farther away. This has a certain amount of logic to it. It's easier to help someone living in your local area. You likely have a better sense of what they need and what resources are available to them.

I've often wondered why we're so eager to help people in Kenya, for example, when there are so many in need right in our own country. I've come to believe that this is the wrong question to ask. A better one might be:

Where and how is God calling me to help? What has He put in my heart?

Some people prefer to work in animal charities. Should we look down on them because they're not helping humans? I don't think we have that authority.

> Worry about the future often interferes with loving our neighbor. We worry about having enough to care for ourselves and our families.

In Paul's first letter to the Corinthians (1 Cor. 12:1–31), he makes this point with the human body analogy. We can't all be eyes. Otherwise, the body wouldn't function. God has given us different gifts so that we can help other parts of His Creation.

So, what can you do to share His love? How, and how much, can you give? I think that there are four principles you should follow:

1. **Give first.** Don't wait until the month's end so that you can give whatever is left over. By giving

first, whether of your time, talent, or treasure, you are honoring the philosophy of Proverbs 3:9, which says:

Honor the lord with your possessions, and with the firstfruits of all your increase.

I like that this forces us to be more dependent on the Lord. You've given expectantly and now have to believe that God will provide for your needs if you run short at the end of the month.

2. **Give proportionally.** It took us a long time to get to the expected 10 percent tithe. I was always one of those who made the "gross or net?" argument. My lack of faith kept me from making either for many years. Admittedly, it seems like the tax collectors are digging deeper into our pockets every year, and we're far above the 3–5 percent that Roman citizens were believed to pay. Still, God wants us to give and assures us that it will be rewarded (see Malachi 3:10). I struggle with this frequently. I try to support the Kingdom of Heaven in my giving, but I often feel like I'm keeping one foot on Earth and holding back money "for a rainy day."

3. **Give sacrificially.** This is uncomfortable for most of us, and it should be. You're probably not giving

enough if you never have to go without something.

Look at your budget. How much can you trim from that? Our big weakness is eating out. I'm not talking about fancy dinners with expensive bottles of wine and five-course meals. We mostly eat out at

The poorest Americans give the highest percentage of their income to charity—around 12% for those who make less than $25,000 per year.

"The Average American's Charitable Donations: How Do You Compare?" The Motley Fool, accessed May 19, 2025, https://www.fool.com/retirement/2016/11/27/the-average-americans-charitable-donations-how-do.aspx

places where you walk up to the counter to order and pump your ketchup into little paper bowls. Our big splurge is Mexican food on Friday night. Even so, we could easily trim one or two weekly meals from our dining out habit and give $50 more. Giving something up to someone needy is much more satisfying than upsizing your combo meal and stoking up on fries.

What if someone gave you money to donate? It wouldn't be any different for the recipient, but it might be for you.

In 2 Samuel 24, David has (again) angered the Lord and brought a plague down on his people. To stop the plague, Gad tells David to build an altar and make an offering on the threshing floor of Araunah the Jebusite. Araunah offers all that he has for the offering, but David insists on paying:

But the king replied to Araunah, "No, I insist on paying you for it. I will not sacrifice to the lord my God burnt offerings that cost me nothing" (2 Sam. 24:24, NIV).

I think God wants us to give from what we have, not from the coffers of others. Look how Christ reacted to the widow who gave her only two mites:

As Jesus looked up, he saw the rich putting their gifts into the temple treasury. He also saw a poor widow put in two very small copper coins. "Truly I tell you," he said, "this poor widow has put in more than all the others. All these people gave their gifts out of their wealth; but she out of her poverty put in all she had to live on" (Luke 21:1–4, NIV).

I continue to struggle with this. I pray I'm getting better, but I often see myself holding back.

4. **Give cheerfully.** Even little children know the difference between a sibling happily sharing and one who has to give up

> Cheerful giving isn't just about the money or time you donate, it's also about being grateful for the ability to give.

a toy "because Mom said so." Paul said it nicely in his second letter to the Corinthians:

Remember this: Whoever sows sparingly will also reap sparingly, and whoever sows generously will also reap generously. Each of you should give what you have decided in your heart to give, not reluctantly or under compulsion, for God loves a cheerful giver. And God is able to bless you abundantly, so that in all things at all times, having all that you need, you will abound in every good work. As it is written:

"They have freely scattered their gifts to the poor; their righteousness endures forever" (2 Cor. 9:6–9, NIV).

Cheerful giving touches on one of the things that bothers me about anonymous giving. You don't see the impact when you give to a large charity. Sometimes, even when you give to your church, it feels impersonal. I don't need my name inscribed on a brick. What helps is connecting with those in need and seeing that I have helped them directly.

Christ didn't endow a charity with a billion gold talents so that we could draw on that account to pay for our sins. He gave His life in exchange for those sins — ours and all who believe in Him. His was a check written in blood for Christians throughout time. He didn't just pay when He died on the cross; I think He pays every day for every sin. His love is immense, and we only receive it because He freely gives it.

Discussion

1. Is there a natural order for whom to help first? If so, what is it?

2. Is it okay to withhold money from your church if your leadership has taken a stance you disagree with? Are there better ways to have your voice and opinions heard?

Exercise

Take an honest look at your finances and spending. Are you giving proportionally? Are you giving anything? Do you give first?

SESSION 6

Running Laps

Shortly before the rains began, the first coach was born. He probably made Noah's kids run laps. Forgot to clean the elephant pen? Give me five laps around the ark, then clean the pen. Sass your elders? Ten laps. Forgot to load the unicorns? That'll be fifteen.

Laps were training disguised as punishment. I ran more than my share. I even joined the track team, where the workouts and

> Practice makes perfect, but nobody's perfect, so why practice?
> Because it makes you better. Practice pushes you closer to the ideal.

punishment for goofing around were the same: laps. Maybe the coach had a limited bag of tricks.

As I've gotten older, I've thought that much of adult life is like running laps—we do many repetitive things, even if it's not running around a 400-meter oval. We endure the pain and tedium of learning a new skill (or job) and get better at it. Sometimes, we make the same mistakes in the second year as in the first. It doesn't mean we're idiots or incompetent; the work can be difficult, and we need more practice.

Professional quarterbacks make occasional bad throws, and a pass is intercepted. Concert violinists miss a note and get a bad review. It's part of the human experience. Why should Christianity be any different?

Just as childhood prepares us to be adults, being an adult Christian should prepare us for eternity in God's presence.

What are the Christian equivalents of running laps— things we should do routinely to get better?

- Confession
- Gratitude
- Loving our neighbors
- Submission to God's will (trusting God)
- Forgiveness
- Behaving like a Christian
- Others?

We discussed confession in Session 3, so we won't discuss it again here. Remember that confession is not a "once and done" thing. As a human, you're likely to continue to sin. Confess and hand those sins over to Christ routinely.

Practicing Gratitude

We are richly blessed, and acknowledging that with gratitude rejuvenates our spirit and makes us better able to show Christ to the world. Here are some ways to cultivate gratitude:

- **Gratitude journaling**: I don't keep a specific journal for gratitude, although it seems like a good idea and a wonderful thing to pass on to your children. I write myself a lot of reminders in a notebook: work tasks, doctor's appointments, and book/movie suggestions. This Lent, I'm adding things I'm grateful for in the hopes that I'll remind myself when I review my notes. Write down specific things you are thankful for, focusing on significant and minor aspects of your life.

> God has given us a world full of beauty and love. Sometimes we just need to look a little harder to see it.
>
> Just because something is hard doesn't mean it's not worth doing.

- **Mindful moments:** Pause throughout the day to consciously acknowledge positive experiences and sensations. Stop and smell the roses. Admire the flowers or the smell of fresh-cut grass. Take a minute to breathe deeply and remember your blessings.

- **Expressing thanks:** Tell people you appreciate them verbally or through a handwritten note. First responders and military personnel put their lives and safety on the line for us. Thank them.

- **Gratitude walks:** My close friend, Gary, gave me this idea. Walking his dog every morning and evening, he thinks about what he's grateful for. What beauty and simple pleasures have been apparent in your day? These walks are also a perfect time for prayer.

- **Share gratitude with others:** Talk to friends and family about what you are thankful for, particularly when it's them.

- **Pay it forward:** Show appreciation through thoughtful actions for others. Things that seem small to you can be a great help to others. Return someone else's shopping cart. Help them load their car. Pick up something they've dropped. Be thankful to people who make your life easier— the delivery people, medical professionals, and restaurant workers. Maybe they're having a bad day, and your kindness will turn it around.

Loving your neighbor was covered in Session 5. Just remember that this is a lifelong exercise. Even when they vote for a candidate you can't stand or invade Ukraine, you're still expected to love them. You don't have to like what they do, but they are still children of God.

Submission to God's Will

Ugh. Do I have to? Yes (James 4:7).

My dictionary defines *submission* as "the action or fact of accepting or yielding to a superior force or to the will or authority of another person."[18]

Hmm . . . "Superior force" sounds like God. Okay, so how do I submit?

- **Start with prayer:** See Session 4. Add your intent to submit to God's will to your prayers. I think He'll be happy to help.

- **Bible study:** Try to read your Bible every day. Think about what you've read. Do a Bible study with your small group or online. If you're like me, you'll find things that hit you right between the eyes in books and verses you've read before.

---

[18] *The Oxford American College Dictionary* (G. P. Putnam's Sons, 2002), under "submission."

- **Humility:** As Clint Eastwood said in *Magnum Force*, "A man's got to know his limitations." We've all got them. Recognizing our limitations and

> Admitting our weaknesses and failings—even if it's just to ourselves—opens the door to Christ a little wider.

dependence on God allows us to acknowledge that His wisdom surpasses ours, and we might as well get used to it.

- **Surrender:** This terrifies me and is one of my biggest spiritual challenges. I know I need to trust God more, but I don't understand why it's so hard for me. I'm a work in progress. Try to intentionally relinquish control of your life, trusting God's plan even when it's unclear.

- **Seek guidance:** I do pretty well in asking God for direction in important decisions and seeking His will before making choices. Where I fall down is listening to His answers. I find myself so wrapped up in the hustle and bustle of life that I don't take the time to be quiet enough to hear that still, small voice.

- **Obedience:** Maybe if I listened, I'd be better at obedience. The good news is that what God wants from us is already written down and easy to reference. My tendency to obey skyrockets when

I force myself to think about God's teachings and commands.

- **Service:** Christ washed His disciples' feet and told them they

> Service opportunities abound. Look for volunteer opportunities near you through your church or on the internet.

should do the same (John 13:14–15). Humble yourself and submit to God by serving others. Check out Gale Sayers's book, *I Am Third,* for inspirational reading outside the Bible. Sayers's philosophy is that God is first, others are second, and he is third. Volunteers are always needed at homeless shelters, food banks, and schools. I recently discovered an opportunity to serve by working with search dogs—essentially playing hide-and-seek with dogs trained to find lost people.

Submission is not unthinking obedience. It's about using your gifts and trusting God's plan. Like the other topics in this session, it should be an ongoing activity, not a single event.

The next session will cover forgiveness. More than any other topic, forgiveness is about running laps and working with Christ to let things go.

John Wesley's Covenant Prayer puts it nicely:

"I am no longer my own, but thine.
Put me to what thou wilt, rank me with whom thou wilt.
Put me to doing, put me to suffering.
Let me be employed by thee or laid aside for thee,
Exalted for thee or brought low for thee.
Let me be full, let me be empty.
Let me have all things, let me have nothing.
I freely and heartily yield all things
To thy pleasure and disposal.
And now, O glorious and blessed God,
Father, Son, and Holy Spirit,
Thou art mine, and I am thine. So be it.
And the covenant which I have made on earth,
Let it be ratified in heaven. Amen."

Behaving like a Christian

The worst thing about Christianity is Christians.

Not all of us, but enough.

Christians are seen as hypocrites, anti-homosexual/LGBTQ+, authoritarian, judgmental, nationalist, smug, self-righteous, anti-abortion, pushy, and intolerant.[19]

---

[19] "Criticism of Christianity," Wikipedia, accessed March 5, 2025, https://en.wikipedia.org/wiki/Criticism_of_Christianity.

There are more—and more hateful—descriptions of Christians, but you get the point.

The sad thing is that we've all seen it. So, how can we be better Christians?

1. Remind yourself daily what your goal is—to be more connected to Christ and seek and heed

> Your walk as a Christian begins the moment you accept Christ and does not end on this Earth. Ever.

   His guidance. Read your Bible and think about what you've read. This will help you follow God and be more successful on your path (Josh. 1:8).

2. Live your faith. Anger and a sharp tongue are significant spiritual weaknesses in my life. When I'm patient and consciously trying to show love and kindness to others, I'm helping us both. Remember what Jam es said: *But be doers of the word, and not hearers only, deceiving yourselves* (James 1:22).

   As I looked for that verse, I read further and got smacked in my heart by this: *If anyone among you thinks he is religious, and does not bridle his tongue but deceives his own heart, this one's religion is useless* (James 1:26).

3. Practice forgiveness and grace—more on this in Session 7.

4. Be part of the Christian community. This is more than just going to church and small groups. That is important, but insufficient. We need to be seen by the world that does not know Christ. Show the world Christ's love through your kindness to those in physical or spiritual need and . . .

5. Share the Gospel. I don't mean that you should go cubicle-to-cubicle proselytizing at work. Share your faith through words and actions. As Christ said in Matthew 28:19–20: *"Go therefore and make disciples of all the nations, baptizing them in the name of the Father and of the Son and of the Holy Spirit, teaching them to observe all things that I have commanded you; and lo, I am with you always, even to the end of the age."*

    I love how Christ ends that verse with a reminder that we're not alone in this.

6. Obey God. Jesus said: *"If you love Me, keep My commandments"* (John 14:15).

    We want our kids to do what we tell them to do. When they fail, we want them to do what I think God wants us to do in the same situation—try harder to avoid making the same mistake, be sorry when you fail, and always strive to be the best Christian you can be.

7. Judge yourself first. Before judging anyone else, reread Matthew 7:1–5. We are often blind to

> Judge not, that you be not judged.
> (Matt. 7:1)

the planks in our own eyes. Pray before judging anyone else, and remember that being judgmental is one of the most significant issues that drives people away from Christians.

Your Christian path is a lifelong one. Every day brings a new opportunity to connect yourself and others to Christ.

Discussion

1. What are your spiritual blind spots? What are the planks in your own eyes? How can we remove them?

2. What have you thought, said, or done today that would give Christians a bad name? What can you do in the future to be a better example?

3. What repetitive actions (laps) help you be a better Christian?

4. James 2:17 is often a point of contention among Christians. Read it and discuss it.

5. After you've done the above, read James 2:18–26. Does that alter your perception of the argument?

Exercise

1. Take a few minutes before bed to write a list of what you're grateful for—just for that day. Try this for a week, then look at how your list has grown and changed. The more we acknowledge what God and others have done for us, the more we realize how surrounded we are in love.

2. How can you be more connected to the Christian community? Consider opportunities both inside and outside of your church.

SESSION 7

Forgiveness

Forgiveness is sometimes difficult to put into words. A friend of mine recently asked me what it means. An hour later, we were still talking about it. Forgiveness involves willfully putting aside feelings of resentment toward someone who has committed a wrong, been unfair or hurtful, or otherwise harmed you in some way. It is not merely accepting what happened or ceasing to be angry. Rather, it involves a voluntary transformation of your feelings, attitudes, and behavior, so that you are no longer dominated by resentment and can express compassion, generosity, or the like toward the person who wronged you.

On Palm Sunday, we celebrate Christ's triumphal entry into Jerusalem and then run smack into Holy Week and a lot of reminders of the pains Christ endured for us. When I was younger, we called Holy Thursday "Maundy Thursday." Kind of an odd name, and I don't remember being told why we called it that.

Maundy Thursday is the day we remember the Last Supper. We all know the rituals and words we hear, but reread John 13–16. There's a lot of stuff in those chapters—I feel His humanity. Christ was very talkative that evening. It's as if He were a parent about to leave the kids home alone for a while, and lots of things were popping into His mind that He wanted them to remember while He was away. The most important was possibly a new commandment.

> Maybe we should have kept the term *Maundy Thursday*—or better yet—call it *Mandate Thursday* to remember Christ's new commandment.

"Maundy" comes from the Latin *mandatum* (a mandate or command) and refers to the commandment Christ gave us in John 13:34:

"A new commandment I give to you, that you love one another; as I have loved you, that you also love one another."

Take a moment to consider that. He's not just saying to love one another. He's saying to show each other the kind of love He showed us. There's a big difference.

As we enter Holy Week, I try to think about what I would have done if I'd been in Jerusalem when Christ was crucified. Would I have been a disciple? Would I have denied Him? Would I have betrayed Him?

Would I have been blind to the arrival of the Messiah?

I probably would have been a Pharisee. A religious, rule-following zealot, screaming for the crucifixion of our Lord. It horrifies me.

He must have been in horrible pain, and yet one of the last things He said was:

"Father, forgive them, for they do not know what they do" (Luke 23:34).

Dying on a cross, mocked by many, and having people gamble for his clothing, Christ *forgave*. That's the kind of love He commands us to give.

> Even as He died on the cross, Jesus loved us so much that He forgave those who crucified Him.

Why, then, is it so hard for me? For us?

Holding a grudge may be my superpower. I understand the emotions behind the Hatfield-McCoy feud. I'm still struggling to forgive things that happened to me years ago. I work on it almost every day and feel myself slowly inching closer, only to wake up some mornings and feel as if I'm back at the start.

The Power of Forgiveness

Forgiveness is one of the most potent and transformative acts we can practice. It is not just an emotional

> Resentment is like drinking poison and then hoping it will kill your enemies.
> —Nelson Mandela

response but a deliberate and conscious choice that leads to healing, peace, and spiritual growth. The Bible repeatedly emphasizes the importance of forgiveness, not only for those who are forgiven but also for those who offer it.

It is central to our faith. Jesus stressed the necessity of forgiving others in the Lord's Prayer:

"Forgive us our trespasses, as we forgive those who trespass against us" (Matt. 6:12).

God's forgiveness is inherently linked to our willingness to forgive others. When Peter asked Jesus,

"Lord, how often shall my brother sin against me, and I forgive him? Up to seven times?"

Jesus said to him, "I do not say to you, up to seven times, but up to seventy times seven" (Matt. 18:21–22).

Christ then told the Parable of the Unforgiving Servant (Matt. 18:23–34) and finished with this:

"So My heavenly Father also will do to you if each of you, from his heart, does not forgive his brother his trespasses" (Matt. 18:35).

The Importance of Forgiveness

1. Emotional and Psychological Healing

- Holding onto resentment and grudges leads to emotional distress, including anxiety, depression, and bitterness.

- Forgiveness allows individuals to release these burdens and experience inner peace.

- Research has shown that forgiveness therapy can help reduce stress and promote overall well-being.

2. Physical Health Benefits

- Chronic anger and resentment have been linked to high blood pressure, heart disease, and weakened immune function.

- Forgiving others helps lower stress hormones and improves physical health.

> Without Christ, I am not strong enough to forgive those who I think have wronged me.

- The act of forgiveness has been linked to lower levels of cortisol, the primary stress hormone, resulting in improved overall health.[20]

3. Spiritual Growth and Strengthening Faith

- Forgiveness deepens our relationship with God by aligning us with His divine nature.

- Jesus set the ultimate example of forgiveness when He forgave those who crucified Him.

- When we forgive, we open our hearts to God's grace and strengthen our faith.

How to Practice Forgiveness

1. Acknowledge the Hurt

- Forgiveness does not mean ignoring or excusing wrongdoing.

- Recognizing the pain caused by others is an essential step toward healing.

2. Pray for Strength and Guidance

- Ask God for the strength to forgive, even when it feels impossible.

---

[20] "Forgiveness: Your Health Depends on It," Johns Hopkins Medicine, accessed March 7, 2025, https://www.hopkinsmedicine.org/health/.

- Seek comfort in Scriptures that emphasize God's mercy and love.

3. Let Go of Resentment

- Understand that forgiveness is a choice, not a feeling.
- Release the desire for revenge or retribution and trust in God's justice.

4. Extend Grace and Compassion

- Remember that we are all sinners in need of God's grace (Rom. 3:23).
- Show kindness and understanding to those who have wronged us.

5. Seek Reconciliation When Possible

- If safe and appropriate, communicate with the person who has wronged you.
- Approach reconciliation with humility and love, but accept that some relationships may never be fully restored.

6. Embrace God's Forgiveness for Yourself

- Many of us struggle with self-forgiveness and carry guilt and shame for our mistakes.

> When you forgive someone, all of that space the resentment occupied in your brain is now free to be filled with God's love and joy.

- Accept that God's mercy is boundless and trust in His promise: If we confess our sins, He is faithful and just to forgive us our sins and to cleanse us from all unrighteousness (1 John 1:9).

I understand Joseph forgiving his brothers (Gen. 50:15–21) and Stephen forgiving those who stoned him to death (Acts 7:59–60). The one I never understood until I became a parent was the Parable of the Prodigal Son (Luke 15:11–32).

You're the dutiful son; you've done all the right things while your brother has gone off and squandered his inheritance on reckless and extravagant living. I'd have been upset to see my brother return to a celebration as I worked in the fields. Now, I look at my daughters and understand the joy a father would feel if a lost child returned.

The Transformative Power of Forgiveness

When we practice forgiveness, we experience a profound transformation:

- Our hearts become lighter, free from the burden of bitterness.

- We develop a deeper connection with God, mirroring His love and mercy.

- We create an environment of peace and harmony in our relationships.

The Mayo Clinic says forgiveness brings peace, happiness, and emotional and spiritual healing. Forgiveness can take away the power the other person continues to have in your life.[21]

Forgiveness is not always easy, but it is essential for a fulfilling Christian life. It fosters healing, enhances our well-being, and strengthens our faith. Following Jesus's example, we open our hearts to God's grace and allow His love to flow through us. Whether forgiving others, seeking forgiveness, or learning to forgive ourselves, embracing this divine principle brings true freedom and spiritual growth. As Ephesians 4:32 reminds us, *And be kind to one*

---

[21] "Forgiveness: Letting go of grudges and bitterness," Mayo Clinic, accessed March 7, 2025, https://www.mayoclinic.org/healthy-lifestyle.

another, tenderhearted, forgiving one another, even as God in Christ forgave you.

Discussion

1. What does it mean to forgive, both from God's perspective and from a human one?

2. What practical steps can we take to forgive others, even when it's difficult?

Exercise

1. Try to understand the other person's perspective and the circumstances that led to the hurt. Is it possible that you misunderstood something? Who needs to forgive you?

2. Write a forgiveness letter. Please do not send it, but let your feelings out onto the page to help you process the pain and anger you feel. Write everything you've wanted to say. Then burn the paper and pray for God to help you forgive.

About the Author

Pat Daily is a mediocre Christian who is trying to get better. He was raised in the Episcopal Church and served as an altar boy in his youth. For much of his life, he has stayed on the periphery of his faith.

As a husband and new father, he had an epiphany when his wife told him, "You need to be the spiritual leader of this family."

That question led him to question how he practiced his faith and what it really meant. Naturally curious, he wondered why we do many of the things we do as Christians and how they evolved.

Following a vapid small group study of Lent, he launched this project to find out how Lent started and why some denominations don't practice it at all. This book is the result.

Pat is also an engineer and former Air Force test pilot who worked at NASA's Johnson Space Center on both the Space Shuttle and International Space Station programs. He is currently working in experimental flight test projects for electric- and hydrogen-powered aircraft, and is the author of the Spark Chronicles science fiction series.

He strongly believes that you can be both a scientist and a Christian and that when the two disagree, it simply means that we don't yet understand either adequately.

Pat and his wife live in Houston and are members of John Wesley Methodist Church.

See his blog at: https://thepatdaily.com.

Also by Pat Daily

The Spark Chronicles (Fiction)

Book 1 – Spark

Boundary Layer Books, Second Edition, 2022

Book 2 – Fire

Boundary Layer Books, 2022

Book 2.5 – OrcLand, a Spark Chronicles novella

Boundary Layer Books, 2023

Book 3 – Embers

Boundary Layer Books, 2025

Acknowledgements

Thanks to all who read early versions of this and/or attended my first teaching of this study:

My wife, Ardith.

The Growing Christians Sunday School class at John Wesley Methodist Church.

Kathleen Schaeffer

Gary Hecker

www.ingramcontent.com/pod-product-compliance
Lightning Source LLC
Chambersburg PA
CBHW031243120626
46545CB00007B/2623